LONDON IN COLOR

LONDON

in Color

INTRODUCTION BY NEVILLE BRAYBROOKE

A STUDIO BOOK

THE VIKING PRESS . NEW YORK

LIBRARY OF CONGRESS CATALOG CARD NUMBER 61-8062

First published, 1961

© NEVILLE BRAYBROOKE, 1961

MADE AND PRINTED IN GREAT BRITAIN
BY JARROLD AND SONS LTD, LONDON AND NORWICH
FOR THE PUBLISHERS
THE VIKING PRESS INC.,
625 MADISON AVENUE, NEW YORK 22, N.Y.

CONTENTS

INTRODUCTION

The way to see London is from the top of a 'bus—the top of a 'bus, gentlemen.—Gladstone

I do not search, I find. That is the best spirit in which to approach any great city, and on the eve of beginning this introductory essay I had stood waiting for a bus in Battersea Park Road, outside the Labour Exchange, when my eye was caught by the words: PROGRESS CHASER. I read on. 'One Experienced in Progressing and Controlling Flow of Work through Factory.' It was as if time had slipped back a century, and as I boarded a 170 so the streets seemed to narrow and grow cobbled. This was the London of Mayhew and Dickens—where Vauxhall's groves and lanes had been cut down to make Kennington's byways; where cafés still bore their old names—*The Feedwell* and *Park Eel Shop*; and where timber yards had replaced the famous Nine Elms that had once marked a forest boundary. Against the grey penitential walls of Victoria Dwellings, posters had been slapped advertising a winter circus under a centrally heated big top. Across the road, modern blocks of flats spoke of the new prosperity abroad—Bank Court, for instance, on the edge of Newtown Street and only two minutes' walk from the borough's Public Bath House opened in 1901 by Sir Charles Dilke.

For over everything in this scattered city lie the shadows of contrast. Earlier descriptions still hold—'the busy emporium' of Tacitus and the Venerable Bede's 'mart of many nations', Dunbar's 'flower of cities' and Rasmussen's 'unique city'—but they need to be incorporated in a picture of a metropolis covering over a hundred square miles in which there is little architectural unity and in which the different centuries, like different buildings, overshadow each other. The stops on any bus-route tell their own story: Battersea Labour Exchange; The Lost Dogs' Home; Harleyford Road, behind the Nine Elms goods depot and leading direct to the river; *Fox Hall Restaurant* on the site of the original Vauxhall Pleasure Gardens; the Albert Embankment; *The Old Father Thames*, a tavern preserved, refaced, and set into a large contemporary block of offices; Lambeth Palace, the traditional 'town home' of the Archbishop of Canterbury with its extensive grounds and private park; Crozier Street—the stop for St Thomas's Hospital and the last stop on the 170 route on this side of the river.

As the bus swung over Westminster Bridge, I could see a light burning above the clock face of Big Ben; it meant that Parliament was still sitting. Under a full moon the magnesian limestone glowed with a grey silveriness —a huge towering 'folly' of figures, foliage, and finials that had won first prize for a building in the Gothic style in 1835 and that, by the dying sun, recalls a mad magenta moment of medievalism on the part of its two creators, Pugin, aged forty, and Barry, aged twenty-three. Then, gathering speed, the bus turned east down Victoria Embankment, passing Scotland

8

Yard, a mock baronial highland castle whose architecture presents its own kind of facial justice—the fact that its granite was quarried by convicts. Less than a minute later came Horse Guards Avenue and the terminus.

Looking down this stretch of river from Westminster Bridge, Wordsworth had seen his 'Ships, towers, domes, theatres, and temples lie/Open . . . to the sky'. Yet the skyline that he saw had lost much of the beauty that John Stow records when two centuries earlier the northern waterfront had offered a continuous panorama of sails, belfries, masts, spires, and palaces. The bells of long ago no more ring out pleadingly, joyously, fretfully across the fields of Soho or St James (now both enclosed as squares); nor do the ringers of Ludgate, Cornhill, and Blackfriars send out their clangour of bells in loud dispute, the peals of St John Zachary contrasting clearly with the subdued carillon of St Botolph's Aldgate. The voice of London calling has become symbolized in the voice of Big Ben. In club and café alike the same chimes herald the same news bulletins, linking the long galleried rooms of the Reform in Pall Mall with the *Park Eel Shop* and its pin-tables in Battersea.

Yet conformity in England never means uniformity. There lies its saving grace, preserved in the nonconformist conscience. Moreover, if this sounds a paradox, then that is because to Englishmen conformity is a two-edged word implying independence as well as unity; their history has matched their temperament, and figuratively, no less than literally, their cities, laws, and constitutions have developed as a number of winding ways with loops. The *autobahn* that cuts straight through the past to

9

the present is quite alien to them, and explains why London's citizens have never allowed their capital to be made subject to one architectural plan, however nobly conceived. Nothing came of Wren's clearance schemes in the seventeenth century, and Nash's hopes in the nineteenth of linking Carlton House Terrace with Regent's Park met with only limited support. In each case, compromise and improvisations were preferred. Likewise, after the Great Fire of 1666 and the blitzkreig of the last war, the chances to reclaim the lost lawns and terraces that had once led down to the river were missed because, on each occasion, independent speculators, fighting for their own building interests, exploited the situation. And the name in which they conquered, helped by their fellow-citizens, was private enterprise. For it is a paradox in the British Constitution that public outcry in supporting private enterprise has often in the end to defend itself against private enterprise.

The public gardens along Victoria Embankment fall, partly, under the shadow of the National Liberal Club—an ironic reminder of the battle waged to preserve this slip of green running from Horse Guards Avenue to Waterloo Bridge. These gardens, once threatened by a hotel development scheme, are administered by the London County Council, one of whose by-laws (No. 28) reads: 'No person shall in any open space sort rags, bones, refuse or matter of like nature *or mend any chair*' (my italics). Such by-laws are always printed in minute type and, if read, immediately put a Londoner on the look-out for other such oddities—that pastime which so delighted John Timbs during the 1860s when he was compiling his volumes of *Things Not Generally Known*. At Charing Cross Tube, I found a notice patriotically printed in red, white, and blue: 'Dogs and Push Chairs must be Carried.' It showed a nice sense of propriety, with dogs coming before push chairs, and serving to emphasize how dogs, no less than bishops, have their appointed place in English metropolitan life. The term dog-collar, which might raise cries of anti-clericalism abroad, can at home be used with the best will in the world.

(As I have been writing this last page, a rag and bone man has called at the house opposite; he has collected a rusty electric heater and a brass bedstead; he has also given his horse an apple. Now they are ready to move off. 'Come on, son', I hear him say as he flicks the reins. I am reminded of a holiday spent earlier in Brittany, the journey back and the first thing heard at a cigarette and sweet counter: 'And a quarter of toffees for the dog.' Nothing could have made the contrast sharper between a *tabac* in St Jacut and a tobacco kiosk at Hampstead Tube.)

On the London tubes and on the top decks of buses, dogs and cats may only be carried at the discretion of the conductor. But on train journeys tickets for dogs must be bought. There is an odd discrimination between taking an alsatian from Charing Cross Tube to Hampstead free, and from Charing Cross Southern Railway Station to Croydon— for which the third of an adult's fare is charged. And there is an even odder discrimination in taking a Siamese cat from any main line terminus station. For no such thing as a cat ticket exists, and whether he travels free, or at the price of a dog, lies completely at the discretion of the guard. This loophole in the conditions governing the sale of railway tickets is characteristic: many similar loopholes extend to London County Council by-laws and the enforcement of Law in general.

For more than a century Victoria Embankment Gardens have served as a night refuge for tramps and derelicts. Close to Hungerford Footbridge which runs parallel with Charing Cross (railway) Bridge stood the blacking factory in which Dickens had worked as a boy; and near to Hungerford Footbridge (so aptly christened) and beneath the Charing Cross arches came the voluntary *Silver Lady Canteen* of the thirties, offering hot soup and bread to the poor. Yet it is perhaps indicative of the change of fortune brought about in these parts that the last verse of a well-known hymn is now dropped in the fashionable churches and chapels off the Strand:

> *The rich man in his castle,*
> *The poor man at his gate,*
> *He made them high and lowly*
> *And ordered their estate.*

For the tramps and derelicts that remain in the Welfare State do so more by choice than necessity. They are part of a band of loiterers, vagrants, and idlers who live by keeping within the letter of the Law ('as long as the letter's a loop not a noose you're fine') and by picking up what they can find: the streets may not be paved with gold, but a trained eye can pick anything up to ten shillings in the way of dropped change after an evening rush hour.

Away from the Embankment, their counterpart on the other side of metropolitan life are to be found in the street traders—the hawks and sparrows of Trafalgar Square of Piccadilly: the boys with their barrows banked into pyramids of fruit to catch the sun, or the peddlers of plastic trays, horoscopes, and cures against baldness. And like their predecessors who sold bear's grease to make the dark blonde, twists of saffron and dyes of trotters' oil, they also keep a sharp look-out for the Law, ready to be moved on at any moment 'for causing an obstruction'. For it is against this moving background that the continual drama between the Law and the Artful Dodger has been played—sometimes in deadly earnest, sometimes in scenes of high comedy. *To cop it* is a phrase that suddenly sprang from the back streets after Sir Robert Peel had introduced his police force, just as *leopards* has suddenly sprung up today as a term meaning pimply youths. Both are in the tradition of quick-firing Cockney—like rhyming slang: *steam tugs* for *a bed without bugs*, or *pass the rocking horse* for *pass the bottle of sauce*.

Cockney is the fastest spoken speech in Britain, and is often interpreted by northerners as being a sign of southern sophistication. For London has developed into the most sophisticated city in the world, and musicians and painters in Darlington or Leeds measure the proficiency of their talent by whether or not they are ready to exhibit or play in the capital. London, the clearing-house of Europe and the centre of commerce, has become the show-place of the arts. Just as markets at Billingsgate, Covent Garden, and Smithfield have achieved national status, so the presses of

13

Fleet Street and the golden lights of Shaftesbury Avenue have become the ambition of every provincial journalist or repertory actor (as yet no National Theatre exists—although since 1951 there has been a National Film Theatre on the South Bank close to the Festival Hall).

The 24 bus marked 'Hampstead Heath', which can be picked up at the far end of Horse Guards Avenue, cuts right through the centre of theatreland—and it is a ride hard to beat for both variety and contrast. Overshadowing the Horse Guards stop, stand Westminster Abbey and the Houses of Parliament with their rival towers of Church and State, while ahead lie the rival arts of war and peace, with the National Gallery overshadowing the Admiralty, the War Office, and the whole broad sweep of Whitehall.

In Trafalgar Square itself, bounded by South Africa House on one side and Canada House on the other, the changes in scene are as dramatic visually as they are politically. Here, every Easter Monday, the Aldermaston followers end their three-day march in the cause of nuclear disarmament; here the great issues concerning rail strikes, Labour policy, and Irish partition are argued in public; and here the crackpots, the nervous tics in society to whom London acts as a nerve-centre, plead for the restoration of the Bourbons or birching, or carry banners proclaiming that 'Tomorrow Will be the End of the World'. But when the next day dawns everything is much the same as before. The long 460-foot façade of the National Gallery, with its Grecian portico incorporating columns brought from Carlton House, imposes a pattern of grey and white that is repeated in the plumage of the pigeons that live beneath its parapets. The birds have become city-dwellers, preferring ledges to branches, thereby showing their natural descent from rock doves who breed either in crags or crevices. They are, too, losing the white marking on their wings—another sign of their rock ancestry. Thus it is that photographs taken of the same picture decade by decade show the same scene darkening by day, but growing brighter at night—a paradox typical of urban life. For once dusk comes an ever-increasing number of neon signs are switched on, the globe above the Coliseum Theatre is illuminated, and the white floodlit spray of the fountains falls dazzlingly before the black granite balustrades of this two-acre island pavement. In December, a Christmas tree and crib are set up, the tree being an annual gift from the people of Norway in return for the hospitality shown to their royal family during the Second World War. Yet the rivalry between Church and State never dies, and just as the Long Parliament banned any Christmas festivities in James Park (as the Roundheads abbreviated it), so even as recently as 1959 attempts were made by the Ministry of Works to ban the crib. Puritanism is a state of mind that remains common to all ages.

In 1647 the cross that marked the village of Charing was taken down by an act of Cromwell's Parliament; two centuries later it was replaced. In 1959, when the Vicar of St Martin-in-the-Fields wrote for permission to set up his crib as usual, he received this reply from an official spokesman on behalf of the Ministry:

We sympathize with your object, but the presence of a crib would place an extra burden on the police, and add to their difficulties in controlling crowds at a time when they are already hard-pressed in handling the very large number of Christmas visitors to the Square. Moreover, we feel that the presence of a crib may well provoke controversy and possibly disorder.

The statement showed a curious illogicality in the bureaucratic mind—and Londoners were quick to seize upon it. Why should the police have more difficulties controlling crowds gazing at an ancient Christian symbol than at an illuminated conifer? Letters of protest were sent in by the hundred, speeches were made in the House (the existence of God had once been a party issue in the 1880s), and the matter was taken up in the leader pages of the *Sunday Times*. Public outcry won, the crib stayed, and carols were sung as lustily as before.

Carols are catchy, breeding an infectious jollity in a jostling crowd, and new words are quickly set to familiar tunes. One present version goes:

We three Kings of Leicester Square
Flogging nylons ten bob a pair.

How well the sentiments fit Charing Cross Road at Christmas time, reflecting that mixture of sacred and profane which is the basis of drama and was so regularly a feature of the early dramas in which the audiences would stand in the fields, the actors upon the church steps. Yet today when the old moralities are revived in St Martin-in-the-Fields the medieval element of horseplay is sadly lacking; horseplay has become

16

the province of either the music halls, or the few remaining buskers who nightly entertain the West End cinema queues. Leicester Square has become a scene of musical ghosts—Marie Lloyd, Harry Champion, Nellie Farren: the old variety theatres of the Alhambra and Empire, and Daly's 'the Home of Musical Comedy', have all been pulled down and rebuilt as luxury cinemas. Economics are to blame. Cinemas can run non-stop performances from ten till midnight, whereas theatres can be filled from only three to four hours a day. So it is that rising rents have gradually pushed theatres into small streets such as St Martin's Lane in the case of the New, or else underground as in the case of the Royalty recently opened in the basement of a block of offices erected on the former site of the Stoll Opera House.

London thoroughfares have a habit of imposing invisible barriers. The West End is bounded at one extreme by Oxford Street and, once across it, there is no turning back. Northward from Tottenham Court, the heights of buildings begin to diminish and the distances between the tube stations to increase: Tottenham Court Road, Goodge Street, Warren Street. The names follow like addresses in a directory; they have none of the excitement attached to Hyde Park Corner, Trafalgar Square, or Mansion House; they lack the Norman memories of conquest associated with Theydon Bois (on the Central Line) on the edge of Epping Forest, or the sense of evocation lying in the words Chalk Farm that can still conjure scenes of dairymaids with white pails, even in the depths of a tube tunnel. In 'the square mile' of the City itself, place names can be whole poems—tragical-comical-historical-pastoral: Tower Hill, Threadneedle Street, Steam Packet Wharf, and Plumtree Court. Yet away from the West End or City, or away from the sharp wit of East End alleys (Frying Pan Steps or Limey-Housey Causeway), a sad melancholy invades the ox-red groves and green belt avenues called Norbury and Alma, suggesting curious liaisons between Romford and Enfield. Or what of the curious task facing an index-maker of roads who must put Hercules next to Herbert?

At Mornington Crescent everything changes. Arcadia Works, the home of Craven 'A' Cigarettes, is a crowning achievement of factory architecture. The style is that of an Egyptian temple and it strikes with a sudden freshness after the grey shunting-yards of Euston and the black-grimed dwellings that surround them; at night too it has an added mysterious quality associated with mythology and the Egyptian darkness —something that used to be further emphasized by the two massive bronze cats that guarded the main entrance (although these, alas, have recently been removed to another Carreras' works in Essex). Even so, Arcadia Works remains one of the most successful factories built in the London area—a great white hope for the future and a telling indictment of the dull stone-faced elevations that box in so many miles of the Great West Road. George Cruikshank, who was Dickens's finest illustrator, lived in Mornington Crescent, and I have often wondered if he ever met Tom Sayer on his walks to Camden Town. No. 257 in the High Street where the pugilist lived is now a butcher's.

A charlady of my acquaintance, with a habit of dropping malapropisms, once described Camden Town's populace as a bunch of harlequins; she meant hooligans. Yet both phrases testify to the colour of the life and place. It is a tough neighbourhood, with colonies of Greeks, Cypriots, Jamaicans, and Irish emigrants living side by side, and where the local Catholic church, administered by the Belgian fathers, has the most cosmopolitan congregation of any outside Westminster Cathedral or the Oratory. The most famous public house is *The Mother Red Cap*, which used to be known as the halfway stop between Highgate and Hampstead. Camden Town has also retained its wine shades in which barmen will speak of putting a nob on the fire, regulars will tuck into the biscuits ('They're buckshee, boy'), and where the old trade names on the bottles are still a pleasure to transcribe: Norwich Silk, Holborn Cream, and Crown of Portugal.

Late on Saturday nights after the supermarkets have closed their heavy plate-glass doors, the street markets auction off their fruit, flowers, and fowls; and, later still, the 24 buses become packed with those who have waited more in a spirit of competition than necessity for this final knocking-down. The poverty and hunger which London once knew have almost vanished—though in its place have arisen the problems of age and loneliness. Few die of want, but an old lady's diary that contained nothing save the repeated entry 'Nobody came' offers its own social comment for the 1960s.

The last lap of the journey is a jolting ride, with switchback bridges, sharp corners, and the slow pull of the northern heights beginning to make their effect. Some of the shops still carry their war scars: 'Step Inside—We May Have It', reads one window barricaded since 1940. 'Nazi Insignia Wanted—Best Prices Paid', reads another less than two hundred yards away. Into a landscape of working-men's clubs and derelict church halls new restaurants and Expresso bars have crept, Indian and Italian proprietors competing with the pull-ups and fish and chip caffs that for so long served the coachmen as they still do the bus crews. Hampstead is creeping down the hill, and the increasing number of junk shops that also begin to line the route to Camden Town are indicative of the spreading prosperity. They are a sign for prospectors, signifying first the search to find bric-à-brac to decorate rooms, then for furniture to fill homes. Less than a decade ago, on the books of the estate agents, Hampstead was divided into areas—residential and artisan. That distinction is now fast fading, another aspect of a changing London.

Hampstead terminus lies at the edge of the Heath. At first, penned by railings, the Heath is no more than a spur of land rising towards a cinder track that becomes a site for a fairground on Bank Holidays and that remains a car park for the rest of the year. Opposite, a few village shops straggle to an end; among them there is a bakery with three hooks for leads set in its outer walls, each labelled 'Dog park'.

Dog park and car park—each within yards of the other. Does this give 'the unique city' the claim to be called also the eccentric city? Perhaps. For eccentricity lives by contrast and the last stage of my journey home serves to remind me of the first. The circus whose posters at Battersea I found advertising a centrally heated big top hopes to take Hampstead within its winter circuit. Less than a decade ago Hampstead fair saw the last of the sword swallowers, fire eaters, and strong men because their pitches were taken by fresh attractions—demon cars and flying space ships. Now it seems they may return again, this time under the patronage of the ringmaster. Just as once through the local streets and lanes clowns were sent as heralds to proclaim that the largest herd of Elephants in Europe had arrived on the heath, so today the texts are prophetically rephrased: *Coming Soon!!! A Hundred Tons of Elephants in the Ring at Once!!!* Everything changes, yet everything remains the same.

At the top of the Heath—one of the highest points in London—it is possible to take stock. The night air is sharp, and more than three million lie sleeping in the city below. If the wind is south-easterly it is possible to catch the scent of spray as the tide returns up the Thames estuary. It is a reminder that London is a seaport, and it is this link between sea and port that not only puts its history in one word but explains how the chief port of the Thames has also come to be one of the greatest cities in the world.

My journey from Battersea to Hampstead has lasted an hour. Drawn on a map it shows a curving course, crossing the river, cutting through the West End, skirting the City, and then running straight north. It provides one cross-section of London life—and over half the photographs that follow lie almost directly along its route. Others reach out to Kensington, Chelsea, and Greenwich. Taken as a set these twenty-four pictures present the most important landmarks in the capital, although in each of them much else lies to be discovered because the camera can only show so much. Everybody brings to London what he finds there, and the numerous different adjectives that have been used about it are a testimony to this: wonderful, sophisticated, unique, royal, scattered, eccentric. In Walter Besant's novel, *Lyonesse of Armorel* and in many of his topographical books, he writes of the city as a romantic's dream, whereas George Orwell in his novels and autobiographical books writes of it as a man who knows what it is to be both footweary and slumped on an embankment bench; the first sees London as a city of spires, the second feels that hard stone quality of its endless pavements. On different days, in different moods, at different times, both can be true.

There are three pictures of Trafalgar Square shot from different angles: north and east by day, and north-east by night. Some walking by chance in the Square may find on its parapets the place where the standard British lineal measures are set down—inch, foot, chain, yard, and so on. I do not search, I find. Others seeing the picture of the Royal Exchange may remember how for a season during the Festival of Britain it housed the Mermaid Theatre and brought Kirsten Flagstad out of partial retirement. Now the Mermaid has a permanent home at Puddle Dock, near Blackfriars Bridge. . . . And may this serve as the cue for another word about these photographs. *London must not only be seen to be believed but it must be heard.* That is a guiding principle for looking at its landmarks, and I am reminded of a Mr Know-All whom I overheard say about a battledress production of *Henry V* at the Mermaid: 'You either use the medieval stage, or you use batons and scenery.'

Yet the growth of London, like the growth of the English theatre, reflects a mixture of styles—theatrical and architectural; and likewise actors can be said to be Gothic, and architecture dramatic. In this sense there can be no sharp divisions between buildings and men. Similarly a city is what its citizens make it and Londoners have made London. It is right therefore perhaps that the last word should be given to its children.

The children across the street, a family of five, have placed a ginger cat on the window-sill and are chanting at him: 'Tiger Lily, Tiger Lily'. This is domestic England in the twentieth century with the cat on the hearth; yet it is also Druid Britain and the beginnings of incantation. Dogs and bishops, cats and children, Tiger Lily and the Druids—there is a continuity stretching back across the centuries to worship before a row of trees and worship before a row of stones. Yet words on the air are like straws in the wind; the straws become bricks and cities are built. That is how London came to be and why her buildings can still speak.

The River Thames from Victoria Tower

Looking east towards King's Reach there lie moored the water-buses that in the summer months ply daily between Hampton Court and Greenwich. On the southern bank, in the foreground, stands County Hall, the centre of the London County Council whose administration covers the education, health services, and housing of 28 boroughs. Now there are plans afoot to turn it into a Greater London Council with powers stretching to 52 boroughs, since Greater London includes parts of Kent, Surrey, Essex, and Hertfordshire. In 1951, to celebrate the Festival of Britain, the L.C.C. sponsored Ellenao's crossing of the river on a tightrope just below Hungerford Bridge. He feigned a slip at the last moment—and, true to tradition, gave the crowd the thrill that they had waited for.

The British Travel and Holidays Association

The Houses of Parliament

The new House of Lords was opened in 1847, the new House of Commons in 1850 (its rebuilt Chamber in 1950). The over-all plan was that of Charles Barry, but Pugin was responsible for the bay-windows and oriels, the carved details and sculpture; he also designed the ink-stands and coat-hangers. Yet one great snag remains—the fact that an M.P. is forced to live out of his briefcase; he has no room to call his office and, to fill in his time, he is forced to trudge from Smoking Room to Library, and from Library to Refreshment Room. It was Gladstone who observed that an M.P. could neither relax nor work in the building and must therefore spend the best part of his time waiting for the division bell. Which explains why so many M.P.s have a second profession—finance, journalism, or the Bar.

Fox Photos Ltd

Westminster Hall

Westminster Hall is the most historic building in London. It was begun by William Rufus in 1097, and the roof was carved from Sussex oak in the fourteenth century. 'Probably the finest timber-roofed building in Europe' is the verdict of the Royal Commission—a body not easily given to eulogy. The six statues, at the foot of the stairs, are of Kings, and are examples of good fourteenth-century carving. Tablets on the stairs and in the middle of the Hall mark the places where Wallace, Charles I, and Strafford stood trial, and mark also the lying-in-state of Edward VII, George V, and George VI.

A. F. Kersting, F.R.P.S.

Westminster Abbey

Westminster Abbey stands on the site of an eighth-century 'west monastery'—and hence the derivation of the name Westminster. Later it was rebuilt by Edward the Confessor, enlarged by Henry III and then entirely rebuilt and enlarged by the same sovereign in 1245. Renewal of the outer stonework has gone on ceaselessly ever since, and the present exterior is by no means a faithful copy of the original medieval abbey. At the west entrance, the towers with the gable between were added by Nicholas Hawksmoor in 1739. The Abbey is neither the seat of a bishop, nor a parish church. Like St George's Chapel at Windsor, it shares the distinction of being 'a royal peculiar'. Its jurisdiction falls to a Dean and Chapter whose direct allegiance is neither to the Bishop of London nor the Archbishop of Canterbury, but direct to the Queen herself.

A. F. Kersting, F.R.P.S.

Horse Guards in Whitehall

Here is a trooper of the Household Cavalry on sentinel outside Horse Guards in Whitehall. Some lines by W. E. Henley come to mind:

He wears his inches weightily, as he wears
His old-world armour; and with his port and pride,
His sturdy graces and enormous airs,
He towers, in speech his Colonel countryfied,
A triumph, waxing statelier year by year,
Of British blood and bone and beer.

A. F. Kersting, F.R.P.S.

Trafalgar Square

Of Nelson standing on his stone masthead in Trafalgar Square, Melville once wrote: 'even when most obscured by the London smoke, token is yet given that a hidden hero is there; for where there is smoke, there must be fire'. But, on a fine day, it is worth doubling back to Horse Guards Parade and looking anew at what Melville saw because, with the turning of the century and with the invention of wireless, the interpretation of the hero changes. Above the Admiralty roof, with its conning-towers that can control any part of the Fleet, rises a complicated nest of wire-work, and into this crow's nest, as it were, Nelson suddenly looms into view—the hero of Trafalgar standing amid all the ropes and coils of a modern harbour.

Sound Stills Ltd

The National Gallery

The National Gallery was founded in 1824 with the purchase of 38 paintings, including five by Claude and six by Hogarth. It moved to its present home in Trafalgar Square, designed by William Wilkins, in 1838, and today there are nearly five thousand paintings—of which a changing third remains constantly on exhibition. These paintings have been acquired by purchase, gift, and bequest. In the lobbies to the main hall there are mosaics of a number of contemporaries—sportsmen, film stars, and ballet dancers. During the blitzkreig lunchtime concerts were held, and, in a city under fire, to hear the fugues of Bach and the songs of Schubert was an unforgettable experience; a triumph for the arts of peace over those of war. In the slip gardens, on either side of the portico, fig trees flourish.

A. F. Kersting, F.R.P.S.

36

Trafalgar Square at night

James Gibbs, the architect of St Martin-in-the-Fields and a follower of Sir Christopher Wren, studied for the Catholic priesthood and later joined the Church of England; and just as within St Martin's walls there is a confusion between Roman decoration and Anglican liturgy, so its exterior shows a similar confusion between steeple and Corinthian portico, church and temple. Recent vicars have been household names—Dick Sheppard, Pat McCormick, and Eric Loveday. In the crypt stands a whipping-post of the 1750s—a relic curiously at odds with the spirit of a place that has become famous through a century for its charity towards the homeless. The parish magazine (though it is far from being parochial in a bad sense) is called the *St Martin's Review* and sells ten thousand. At Christmas, special midday services of carols are held for city workers.

The British Travel and Holidays Association

St Clement Danes Church

St Clement Danes, which marks the beginning of Fleet Street, is a Wren church whose steeple is the work of James Gibbs; and its association with St Martin's is famous in nursery rhyme:

> *Oranges and lemons,*
> *Say the bells of St Clement's.*
>
> *You owe me five farthings,*
> *Say the bells of St Martin's. . . .*

The oranges and lemons may derive from the fact that the berths for unloading citrus fruit used to be near London Bridge—though in that case St Clement's Eastcheap would have the stronger claim to the song. A more probable derivation is the fact that porters carrying fruit to near-by Clare Market had to pay a toll to those living at St Clement's Inn. Anyway, the next verse is the cue to turn to the next page:

> *When will you pay me?*
> *Say the bells of Old Bailey. . . .*

A. F. Kersting, F.R.P.S.

The Lord Mayor's Coach at the Law Courts

The Old Bailey is the Central Criminal Court for major trials —murder or treason; but much nearer to St Clement Danes, across the road, stand the new Law Courts serving the three divisions of Chancery, Queen's Bench and Probate as well as Divorce and Admiralty. In the photograph opposite the Lord Mayor's coach brings colour and pageantry to a building which, though competent and consistent in its adaption of an English thirteenth-century style, has never won much popular enthusiasm. One explanation may lie in the gloom of its interior, a gloom not only matching the mood of those brought to trial but also the mood of its last-century architects to whom there was no such thing as shades of crime. To Blomfield and Street, even before the verdict was given, court rooms were little different to cells; and the original plans of 1866, though slightly modified in execution, bear a striking resemblance to those of a prison.

The British Travel and Holidays Association

St Paul's Cathedral

At the top of Ludgate Hill, St Paul's recalls the days *quand les cathédrales étaient blanches*. On a clear morning the words of Corbusier take wing, and the Portland stone glows with an inner whiteness. This is a moment of seventeenth-century grace contrasting sadly with the long shadows of commerce cast by the nineteenth. Yet to capture this idyllic moment (as both sunlight and photographer have) it is also necessary to see the other side of the negative—that moment of perplexity caught by Dickens's street-sweeper looking at the Cross 'glittering above a red and violet-tinted cloud of smoke'. 'From the boy's face one might suppose that sacred emblem to be . . . the crowning confusion of the great, confused city; so golden, so high up, so far out of his reach. For there he sits . . . everything moving on to some purpose and to one end—until he is stirred up, and told to "Move on" too.'

A. F. Kersting, F.R.P.S.

44

The River Thames from Waterloo Bridge

The halfway point through this set of pictures is a good moment to return to the river. In the distance lie Cannon Street Station and the Tower, and on the southern shore can be seen Barge House Wharf and the tower of the Bankside Power Station. Yet much remains hidden—Billingsgate, Queenhithe Dock, Vintners' Hall, and the City Custom House. For just as only from buses can be glimpsed the secret life of banking houses when they close their doors at three, so only from water-buses can be watched the secret life of the docks hidden behind their high brick walls. On the London reaches of the Thames alone, there are seventy miles of wharf, dock, and quay.

A. F. Kersting, F.R.P.S

46

The Tower of London, the White Tower

The Tower was begun by William the Conqueror with the aim of protecting Londoners from invasion by the river. Since then it has served as a prison, a palace, and a citadel. During the reign of Henry VII part of it became a menagerie, and it was one of the citizens' entertainments to watch a bear being led to the water's edge to catch salmon. It is now over a century since a Thames salmon was caught—although as late as the 1820s the fish sold at Billingsgate were all caught locally.

A. F. Kersting, F.R.P.S.

48

The Tower of London and Tower Bridge

Tower Bridge marks the beginning of the Pool of London and is the last bridge before the sea (between Wapping and Rotherhithe there is a tunnel under the Thames and another at Blackwall). It cost one million and a half pounds to build and it was first crossed in 1894 by the Prince of Wales, later Edward VII; it harmonizes well with the Tower—although, architecturally, its twin medieval towers are something of frauds, their granite faces hiding steel frameworks. On an average the giant bascules, which can be raised hydraulically in a minute and a half, open a dozen times a day; only once has a driver been caught at the moment of opening—and that as recently as three years ago. Steel footways (a hundred and forty-two feet above the water) link the two towers, but, as a result of a number of attempted suicides, these have now been closed to the public.

Sound Stills Ltd

50

The Royal Exchange

The third Royal Exchange (1844) stands on the same grounds as its two predecessors—both destroyed by fire. On its north side runs Cornhill, once a grain-market, later the site chosen for the Bank of England, and subsequently famous for a century as the name of a literary magazine whose first offices had looked out on the Royal Exchange. 'Fancy a *Leadenhall Market Review*', one critic remarked to Thackeray—the original editor of the *Cornhill*. But as a comment it showed a weak memory and few prophetic powers; previously there had been Fielding's famous *Covent Garden Journal*, and within less than sixty years there would be *Temple Bar, Belgravia, The Pall Mall Gazette* and the *Strand*. Today *The Clare Market Review*, edited by students from London University, keeps going the tradition of place-names in journalism that for so long has been a feature of London literary life.

Fox Photos Ltd

The Athenaeum and Waterloo Place

The Athenaeum, in Waterloo Place, was intended to be a club for artists and literary men. Thackeray wrote many of his books there, and its name became associated with the best literary weekly of the Victorian era (the old *Athenaeum* is now incorporated in the *New Statesmen*). Designed by Decimus Burton, its architecture immediately strikes a note of erudition and Grecian beauty; the figure on the porch is Pallas Athene, and the frieze beneath the cornice reproduces that of the Parthenon in Athens. It stands in the centre of clubland—hardly a stone's throw from the centre of theatreland at Piccadilly Circus. (*A warning*. The menus in the dining-room should be read carefully lest the *hommard* pie prove *home-made* pie, which the Belgians wisely call *philosophe*.)

A. F. Kersting, F.R.P.S.

Piccadilly Circus at night

Piccadilly Circus, the centre of the West End entertainment world, has been described as 'the hub of the Empire'. In the middle stands a memorial put up to the seventh Earl of Shaftesbury. He was a well-known Victorian philanthropist and the aluminium figure was intended to represent the Angel of Charity—although, ever since it was unveiled in 1893, it has become known to everyone as Eros. Comparatively peaceful as Piccadilly is in this night scene, on Election, Victory, or Coronation nights the Circus becomes a second inferno, with girls being tossed up in blankets and fireworks bursting everywhere. Eros joins Bacchus.

Fox Photos Ltd

St James's Palace

At the bottom of St James's Street is the four-storied Clock Tower of St James's Palace. The Tudor brickwork has weathered remarkably well—although when fire broke out in 1809 it destroyed the eastern wing. Foreign ambassadors are still accredited *to the Court of St James's*, and the choristers in its Chapel Royal still wear the scarlet and gold costumes that so delighted Holbein. Among its choristers and organists have been William Byrd, Orlando Gibbons, Henry Purcell, and Sir Arthur Sullivan. Up to 1939 Royal Levées were held for gentlemen, but this practice has now been discontinued. Democracy and the Crown have grown closer. At Buckingham Palace the Queen now holds select luncheons to which the more renowned scientists, men of letters, and leaders of opinion are invited.

A. F. Kersting, F.R.P.S.

Buckingham Palace
 A few snatches of song surface in the memory:

 The ladies are partial
 To anything martial . . .

Queen Elizabeth II leaves for the State Opening of Parliament. A few gathered in the crowd remember the days when they were lifted shoulder-high to catch a glimpse of Queen Victoria driving to Westminster. Times change but royal pageantry remains the same.

Radio Times Hulton Picture Library

St James's Park

St James's Park, with its artificial Lake created by John Nash, is one of the finest pieces of landscape gardening in any park; it provides the perfect setting for its three palaces of Whitehall, St James's, and Buckingham. There are many waterfowl in this bird sanctuary—geese, swans, pochard, teal, wigeon, mandarin, and South African shelducks—and recently 'ringing' has taken place. Gulls seen over the Lake have later been reported seen in Germany and Norway. John Evelyn, the diarist, once saw a Balearian crane in Birdcage Walk with a wooden leg whose joint was so accurately made that it could walk with ease. The handywork was that of a soldier. Today some old pensioners still retain the art of making matchsticks into splints, and every year a number of crippled birds are nursed back to health.

The British Travel and Holidays Association

The Royal Hospital, Chelsea

The Royal Hospital at Chelsea is a home for old age pensioners. It was opened in 1689 when nearly five hundred pensioners (in the words of John Evelyn) came to live there 'as in a college or a monastery'. The bronze figure in Roman costume by Grinling Gibbons is of Charles II—the founder of the Hospital. It is sad to prick a legend, but Nell Gwyn did not put the idea into the King's head; the idea came after a royal visit to the Hotel des Invalides in Paris. No pensioner under fifty-five can be admitted. Visitors are welcome, and in the cloistered quadrangles veterans will be heard discussing past campaigns from Ladysmith to Mons with the same enthusiasm they now plan their strategy of *memento mori*—the manœuvres by which they can obtain more sugar in their tea or better their position in the refectory.

A. F. Kersting, F.R.P.S.

Grosvenor Square

In Grosvenor Square taxi-drivers have a saying that English is spoken and American understood. John Adams, the first American minister to Britain, came to live at No. 9 in 1785. For a quarter of a century a new Embassy and Consulate stood on the east side, but now a newer building on the west side has been opened (the architect is Eero Saarinen of American-Finnish extraction). Those on the staffs of the Embassy and Consulate are only offered limited appointments in London lest they wish to become anglicized! The trees retain their pleasant informality as when they were first planted in the eighteenth century, but a straight avenue leading to Franklin D. Roosevelt's memorial shows the influence of the New World on the Old.

A. F. Kersting, F.R.P.S.

66

Kensington Palace

'No other Palace stands so well', said George V of Kensington. It was chosen by William III and enlarged by Wren because the near-by sand-pits eased the Royal asthma. Today, before the Dutch[?] ~~German~~ King's double-life-size figure, stretches one of the most exclusive paths in any park—a path to which children are brought promptly on the stroke of ten by their nurserymaids and as promptly hurried away at twelve; a path in which their games, lacking the gashed vitality of the back streets, are subdued to the blue and grey of their blazers; and a path down which swiftly pedalled limousines now glide where once a fair-haired, blue-eyed girl had ridden her donkey, saying to her friends: 'You must not touch those toys; they are mine; and I may call you Jane, but you must not call me Victoria.'

A. F. Kersting, F.R.P.S.

68

The *Cutty Sark*, Greenwich

South-easterly winds have always made good sailing weather on the Thames, and at Greenwich Pier lies the *Cutty Sark* dry-docked in a permanent berth. She was launched in the Clyde less than a century ago; now she has become a *museum piece*. She was the last of the clippers, and soon the last of the sailing barges will become *redundant*. *Museum piece* and *redundant*: these are utilitarian terms in which history is pre-packaged or measured by weight. They are the words of the publicity hand-out, testifying nothing to the spirit of the crews who manned these craft. Which is its own parable. For men master the seas and governments are their ships of state, and upon this twofold principle nations have either ruled the waves or sunk. Sea-power has been half the reason for London's might.

A. F. Kersting, F.R.P.S.

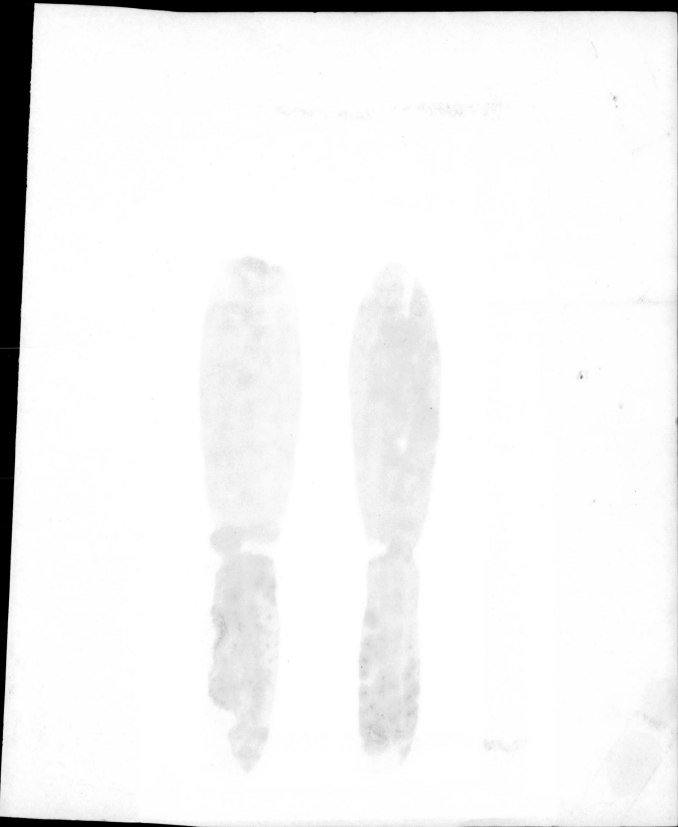